Ready for School
We Are a Team

Listos para ir a la escuela
Somos un equipo

Sharon Gordon

Marshall Cavendish
Benchmark
New York

We are a team.

Somos un equipo.

We work together.
We are a team.

Entrenamos juntos.
Somos un equipo.

We make a plan.
We are a team.

❖

Hacemos planes.
Somos un equipo.

We do our jobs.

We are a team.

———— ❖ ————

Tenemos distintas posiciones.

Somos un equipo.

We take turns.
We are a team.

Nos turnamos.
Somos un equipo.

We do our best.

We are a team.

❖

Damos lo mejor de nosotros.

Somos un equipo.

We help each other.
We are a team.

❖

Nos ayudamos los
unos a los otros.

Somos un equipo.

15

We cheer.
We are a team.

❖

Nos alentamos.
Somos un equipo.

We are friends.
We are a team!

❖

Somos amigos.
¡Somos un equipo!

We Are a team

Somos un equipo

best
lo mejor

cheer
alentar

friends
amigos

help
ayudar

20

jobs
posiciones

plan
hacer planes

take turn
turnarse

work
entrenar

Index

Índice

About the Author
Datos biográficos de la autora

Sharon Gordon has written many books for young children. She has always worked as an editor. Sharon and her husband Bruce have three children, Douglas, Katie, and Laura, and one spoiled pooch, Samantha. They live in Midland Park, New Jersey.

Sharon Gordon ha escrito muchos libros para niños. Siempre ha trabajado como editora. Sharon y su esposo Bruce tienen tres niños, Douglas, Katie y Laura, y una perra consentida, Samantha. Viven en Midland Park, Nueva Jersey.

23

With thanks to Nanci Vargus, Ed.D. and
Beth Walker Gambro, reading consultants

Marshall Cavendish Benchmark
99 White Plains Road
Tarrytown, New York 10591-9001
www.marshallcavendish.us

Library of Congress Cataloging-in-Publication Data

Gordon, Sharon.
We are a team = Somos un equipo / Sharon Gordon. — Bilingual ed.
p. cm. — (Bookworms, ready for school = Listos para ir a la escuela)
Includes index.
ISBN-13: 978-0-7614-2436-9 (bilingual edition)
ISBN-10: 0-7614-2436-9 (bilingual edition)
ISBN-13: 978-0-7614-2357-7 (Spanish edition)
ISBN-10: 0-7614-1994-2 (English edition)
1. Sports for children—Juvenile literature. 2. Teamwork (Sports)—Juvenile literature. 3. Cooperativeness—Juvenile
literature. I. Title. II. Title: Somos un equipo. II. Series.

GV709.2.G6713 2006
796.083—dc22
2006018277

Spanish Translation and Text Composition by Victory Productions, Inc.
www.victoryprd.com

Photo Research by Anne Burns Images

Cover Photo by *SuperStock*/Banana Stock

The photographs in this book are used with permission and through the courtesy of:
Corbis: pp. 1, 11, 21 (bottom l) LWA-Dann Tardif; pp. 3, 9, 21 (top l) Ariel Skelley; pp. 5, 21 (bottom r) Patrick Giardino;
pp. 13, 20 (top l) Kevin Fleming; pp. 15, 17, 19, 20 (top r), 20 (bottom l), 20 (bottom r) Royalty Free.
SuperStock: pp. 7, 21 (top r) Kevin Radford.

Printed in Malaysia
1 3 5 6 4 2